I0517905

Resilient Heartbeats

A Healing Guide for Single
Moms to Overcome Burnout, Stay
Motivated, and Find Joy Again
Sefi Wells

Novane Publishing, LLC

Copyright © 2025 by Sefi Wells

All rights reserved.

No portion of this book may be reproduced in any form without written permission from the publisher or author, except as permitted by U.S. copyright law.

Disclaimer: This book is for educational and informational purposes only. It is not intended to provide financial, legal, or investment advice. Readers should consult a qualified professional for personalized guidance.

Illustrator: Jeffrey Sutorus

Contents

For the single mothers:

The ones who rise before the sun
and fall into bed long after everyone else is asleep.

The ones who've cried behind closed doors,
then wiped their face and kept moving.

The ones who are both soft and steel,
who carry invisible loads and quiet dreams
and love with everything they have left.

This book is for you.

For every moment you wondered if you were enough;

You were.

You are.

You always have been.

This is your reminder, your mirror,
your rally cry and your place to rest.

I wrote this with you in my heart.
You are not alone anymore.

— *With all my love and respect,*

Sefi Wells

Read This First

You didn't choose this book by accident.

You may have picked it up late at night, after the house got quiet, but your mind didn't.
You may have stumbled across it while searching for something, *anything*, to remind you that you're not the only one carrying so much.

Maybe you're exhausted but can't rest.
Maybe you're doing your best but still feel behind.
Maybe you're scared, or grieving, or quietly angry that this is your life now, and you're not even sure if that's okay to admit.

If any of that sounds like you, let me say it clearly:

This book was written for you.

Not for the polished version of you that shows up to school pick-up with a half-smile and a full to-do list.
Not for the version of you who says "I'm fine" because it's easier than explaining.

But for the *real* you, the one who's strong and soft, brave and breaking, rising and rebuilding all at once.

This is not a book about being better.
It's a book about coming home to yourself.

You Don't Have to Pretend Anymore

You've spent enough time trying to hold it all together.
Trying to be everything for everyone.
Trying to stay motivated, stay patient, stay strong, even when you were unraveling.

You've read advice that felt like guilt trips.
You've listened to people who've never had to walk a day in your shoes.
You've seen the highlight reels and wondered what you were doing wrong.

This isn't that.

This is your space.
A soft landing. A quiet mirror. A firm but gentle reminder that you're doing far more than you realize, and that it's okay to want more than just getting through.

What You'll Find Here

This book doesn't offer five easy steps to fix your life.
Because your life isn't broken, it's complex. It's full. It's heavy and holy and hard and beautiful all at once.

Inside these pages, you'll find:

- Truth without judgment

- Tools without overwhelm

- Reflection without shame

- Permission to rest, to feel, to want, to *be*

Each chapter walks with you through one part of your journey. From guilt and exhaustion to rediscovery and healing. From carrying the invisible load to rewriting your inner voice. From surviving solo parenting to redefining what your empowered, grounded, *real* life can look like.

This isn't a book that expects you to hustle harder.
It's a book that invites you to exhale.

You Are Not Alone Anymore

If you've felt invisible, unheard, overlooked, misunderstood, this is your proof that someone sees you.

You are not lazy. You are not failing.
You are carrying more than most people can imagine.

But you're not just surviving. You're building.
You're becoming.
You're creating a life that doesn't just hold your children, but holds *you*, too.

And you don't have to do it alone anymore.

And when you're ready to take the next small step forward, you'll find worksheets and reflection tools organized and accessible in **Chapter 18: Your Empowered Toolkit**. You don't have to wait until the end to begin using them. They're here to support your process, one breath, one page, one decision at a time.

You'll find the printable versions of these worksheets available online at: https://www.novanepublishing.com/sefi-wells#book-resilient

Let This Be the Start of Something

Start wherever you are.
Pause when you need to.
Cry, highlight, scribble in the margins. Let the pages hold what you've been holding in silence.

There is no right way to walk through this book.

There is only your way.

And wherever that path takes you, know this:

You are enough.
You are allowed to want more.
You are not alone.
You are already becoming.

Let's begin together.

Chapter 1

Welcome to Your New Chapter

Y ou're here. That alone says more about you than you probably realize.

Maybe you've been through a breakup, a divorce, or a decision that changed everything. Maybe you've never had anyone beside you on this journey, and you're still figuring out how to carry it all. Whatever brought you here, let me say this first: **You are not alone.**

This book isn't a lecture. It's not going to preach or push or pretend that all you need is a positive mindset. That's not how life works, and you know that better than most. This is a guide, a companion, a steady hand on your back when everything feels like it might fall apart. It's here to give you practical tools, emotional truth, and just enough light for the step you're on.

We are going to talk about the messy parts. The guilt that creeps in at night. The exhaustion that doesn't go away with sleep. The invisible mental load of being the everything-for-everyone-all-the-time person. We're going to shine a light on the fears you hide even from yourself: **"Am I failing my kids?" "Will I ever feel whole again?" "Is this it for me?"**

And then, piece by piece, we're going to build something stronger. **Not from scratch. From you.** Because everything you need is already there. It's buried under despair, pressure, and exhaustion, but it's there. And this book is here to help you dig it out, clean it off, and believe in it again.

Let's Name It: The Primary Complaint

There's one complaint I've heard again and again from single moms, no matter their background or how long they've been doing this alone:

"I feel overwhelmed and unsupported, trying to do everything by myself."

That sentence is more than frustration. It's a truth wrapped in grief and grit. It's the unspoken fear that one wrong move will unravel the whole house. It's the weight of bills, bedtime routines, grocery lists, work deadlines, emotional labor, and unanswered texts. It's doing all of it while hiding your own tears in the bathroom, because the kids are watching.

You may have tried everything to fix it. Planners. Self-help books. Productivity apps. Prayers. Pep talks. Maybe even therapy. But you still feel like you're climbing a mountain barefoot with a child on your back, and no one offering a hand.

That's what we're going to work on, **not just surviving it, but changing your relationship to it.** This journey isn't about pretending it's easy. It's about learning how to **move forward anyway**, with tools that actually support *you*.

This Is a Place for Your Truth

You don't have to pretend here. Not for the world, not for your family, and not for your kids. You can be tired and strong at the same time. You can be proud of what you've built and still wish someone would help you carry it. You can love your children more than anything and still miss the version of you that existed before life became this hard.

You're allowed to want more. Not just for them. For *you*.

This book won't fix everything, nothing can. But it can walk beside you through the nights when you're not sure if you're doing any of this right. It can hand you small, doable steps when everything feels impossible. It can remind you, over and over, that **you are not failing, you are carrying more than most people will ever understand.**

Before We Begin, Take a Moment

Right now, just for a minute, pause. Breathe. Place your hand on your chest and feel your heart, still beating, still showing up, still trying.

You don't need to be perfect. You just need to be honest.

Let's start with that.

Reflection: *Where Am I Right Now?*

Take a pen, a quiet space (even if it's the bathroom with the door locked), and answer this for yourself:

- What am I carrying right now that no one sees?

- When was the last time I felt supported?

- What do I wish someone would say to me today?

- What am I most proud of, even if no one else sees it?

There are no wrong answers. This isn't for performance. It's for presence.

In the chapters ahead, we'll explore your emotional world, your daily struggles, your finances, your health, your identity, and your dreams. But before we dive into the "how," I want you to know this:

You are worthy of a life that doesn't just drain you. You are allowed to want help. You are allowed to be more than just a role.

This is the beginning of something more. Not a new you, just the real you, finally allowed to rise.

Let's begin.

Chapter 2
You Are Not Broken - You Are Becoming

Let's be honest: there are days when it all feels like too much. Days when you're surviving on caffeine and autopilot, barely remembering if you ate breakfast. When silence feels less like peace and more like a weight pressing against your chest. When the bed feels colder than you expected, not just from the absence of another body, but from the missing warmth of feeling understood. When you're smiling at your kids, holding it together for their sake, but inside, you feel like you're sinking, wondering if anyone can see how much you're carrying just beneath the surface.

On those days, it's easy to believe the lie that something in you is broken.

You're not. You're **becoming**.

Becoming doesn't always look pretty. Sometimes it looks like crying in the car after drop-off. Sometimes it looks like holding it together until 9 p.m., then standing in the kitchen with dirty dishes and a thousand unspoken thoughts. Sometimes it looks like texting "I'm fine" when you're anything but, when your heart is heavy, your mind is racing with worries you don't have words for, and all you want is for someone to read between the lines and understand that "fine" is just a shield you're too tired to lower.

But this isn't the end of your story. It's a chapter. A hard one, yes. But not the last.

When Life Changes, You Change

Maybe you didn't choose this. Maybe someone else's decision flipped your life upside down, leaving you to piece together a new normal with hands that were already full. Or maybe you made the hardest choice of your life, to walk away from something that wasn't healthy, even when the unknown felt terrifying. Maybe it wasn't one big moment at all, but a series of small, painful realizations that added up until you knew you couldn't stay where you were.

Either way, you're here. You're navigating life alone, not because you're weak, but because something inside you knew you deserved more. Something inside you whispered that survival wasn't enough, that you were made for something better.

That doesn't mean you *feel* strong every day.

Sometimes you feel invisible, like no one truly sees the thousand tiny sacrifices you make every single day just to keep life moving. Like the world keeps pulling pieces of you, your energy, your patience, your dreams, while offering little back. Like everyone else has a team, a village, a safety net, and you're out here doing life solo, stitching together courage from the scraps no one notices.

It's easy to believe that if you were stronger, smarter, better, it wouldn't feel so heavy.

But what if the struggle doesn't mean you're failing?

What if it means you are standing right in the center of something sacred, something messy and painful, but also deeply holy?

What if it's not weakness you're feeling, but the growing pains of becoming more grounded, more real, and more powerful than you ever thought you could be?

A kind of strength that doesn't shout to be noticed, but roots deep and holds firm when the storms come.

You Are Still Whole

Even on the days when you feel scattered, stretched thin, and like you're piecing your life together with trembling hands, you are not broken.

You are being remade, reshaped by love, perseverance, and a strength you've built one hard day at a time. You are becoming something fierce, honest, and breathtakingly true, even when it doesn't feel glamorous or strong.

Here's what I want you to know, more than anything: you are still whole, even with the broken pieces.

Wholeness isn't about living a life without cracks or messy days. It's not about the perfect relationship status, a Pinterest-worthy home, or never losing your patience. True wholeness is sitting with the truth of who you are, your strength and your sorrow, your laughter and your exhaustion, and knowing deep down that none of it makes you less.

You may have lost parts of yourself along the way. The version of you who danced barefoot in the kitchen. The one who dreamed about road trips with no set destination. The woman who laughed too loud, who stayed up too late writing poetry, who got excited just planning a Friday night with friends. She's not gone. She's just been buried under the survival mode you never asked for.

You don't need to erase what you've been through to become whole. You don't need to go back to who you were before everything changed. You just need to make space for yourself again, to welcome all the parts of you home.

Stop Trying to Prove Yourself

The world will shout at you to hustle harder, climb faster, do more, as if your worth depends on how much you can carry without crumbling. You already know what you're made of; you live it every single day, in the quiet battles no one else sees.

You don't need to stretch yourself so thin that you become invisible just to prove you're enough. You don't need to run yourself ragged trying to fill every gap so your kids won't feel what's missing. You don't need to hold your breath through the hard moments just to feel worthy of asking for a break.

You are already enough, not because of how much you've done, but simply because you exist, because you're still standing, because you love so fiercely even when you're running on empty.

You don't have to earn rest with exhaustion. You don't have to earn joy by sacrificing your spirit. You don't have to earn love by abandoning yourself piece by piece.

Let this be the moment where you stop racing to prove something to the world, and start remembering the truth: you are already everything you need to be.

Becoming Looks Like This

Becoming isn't always obvious or glamorous.

It's you choosing not to snap at your kids when the weight of the day feels crushing. It's dragging yourself out of bed after a night spent worrying about bills or the future, and pouring cereal for dinner because that's all the energy you can summon, and deciding that's enough.

It's standing in a messy living room, surrounded by toys and unfolded laundry, and choosing compassion for yourself instead of sinking into self-blame.

Becoming is whispering "I'm doing my best" on the days when your best doesn't feel like enough.

It's telling the truth about how tired you are. It's showing up at work, at school pickups, at life, even when you feel like you're running on fumes. It's admitting you don't have all the answers but choosing to keep asking the questions, anyway.

Becoming looks like this moment, you, here, reading these words, daring to believe that even through the exhaustion, the fear, and the doubts, you are still becoming someone brave, beautiful, and worthy.

It looks like refusing to give up on yourself, even when the world feels heavy on your shoulders.

Journaling Prompt: The Version of Me I Miss... and the One I Want to Become

Take a quiet moment and reflect. Write freely, no filters, no edits.

1. *What parts of me have I lost or buried since becoming a single mom?*

2. *What do I miss about who I was before this chapter of my life?*

3. *Who do I want to become—not for my kids, but for me?*

4. *What small step could I take this week to bring that version of me closer?*

There's power in seeing yourself. In naming your desires. In remembering that the woman you want to be isn't out of reach, she's already in you. She's just waiting for the space to rise.

You are not broken.

You are a woman in the middle of becoming.

And I promise you, what's coming will be more honest, more grounded, more beautiful than anything you were ever told to settle for.

Let's keep going.

Chapter 3
The Invisible Load

There's a moment, usually late at night after the dishes are finally done, the homework battles are over, and the house has gone still. It's just you, the hum of the refrigerator, and a weight on your chest you can't quite put into words. A mix of exhaustion, loneliness, and the endless mental to-do list you're too tired to tackle but too wired to forget. In that stillness, you feel every decision you made that day, every problem you solved, every worry you carried alone, all pressing down, all asking for space in a mind that's already overcrowded.

No one saw you wiping up the spilled cereal while trying to sound professional on a work call. No one noticed that you managed to sign the school permission slip, squeeze in paying the electric bill, restock the toilet paper, and calmly navigate your child through an emotional meltdown, all before the clock even struck 10 a.m. And still, somehow, a small voice inside whispers that you didn't do enough. That you should have done more, smiled bigger, stayed calmer. It's a heavy and invisible standard you're holding yourself to, one that no one else even sees.

This, right here, is the invisible load.

It's the never-ending pile of everything you think about, worry over, plan, anticipate, manage, fix, and carry, not just physically, but mentally and emotionally, every single day. It's the dentist appointments you remember, the meltdowns you anticipate, the meals you plan, the bills you juggle, the future you constantly prepare for, often without a single person truly seeing the mental chess game you're playing. It's the weight of carrying a whole world in your head and heart, quietly, constantly, and without anyone stepping in to lighten the load or even acknowledge how heavy it really is.

And it is *exhausting*.

It's Not Just About Doing Everything

Let's get something straight: the invisible load isn't just about staying busy or having a packed calendar. It's about carrying the full, silent responsibility for every moving part of your family's life, even the parts no one else notices. It's knowing that if you forget to schedule the doctor's appointment, no one else will. It's tracking your child's shoe size, remembering the field trip form, sensing when a meltdown is brewing before a single tear falls, and quietly adjusting tomorrow's plans to prevent it.

It's not having anyone to tap in when your brain feels like it's buffering and your body is running on fumes.

You're the project manager of your household. The therapist who soothes broken hearts. The referee breaking up sibling squabbles. The breadwinner keeping the lights on. The nurse patching skinned knees. The scheduler coordinating a hundred moving pieces. The chef, the cleaner, the midnight worrier, and the long-term dreamer, all rolled into one person.

It's not just what you do, it's the unseen mental weight you carry, the constant vigilance, the emotional labor of holding everyone else together while trying not to come undone yourself.

And the truth is, most people don't see that part. They only see the outside: the kids are fed, the house is standing, you're still smiling. But underneath it all, your mind is triaging crises and juggling needs 24/7, without a pause button in sight.

The Mental Checklist You Never Get to Finish

You wake up already listing everything that needs to happen before you even touch the floor with your feet, appointments to schedule, groceries to pick up, homework to double-check, emotions to manage that aren't even your own. And at night, when the world finally quiets down, your mind keeps running through the endless list of everything you didn't get to, the unread emails, the unfolded laundry, the quality time you wish you'd had more of. The checklist never shrinks; it only reshuffles itself, asking for more from a heart and body already stretched thin.

- "I need to follow up on that school email."

- "Did I forget to move the laundry?"

- "What are we doing for dinner tomorrow?"

- "Did my child seem off today?"

- "When's the last time I had a moment for myself?"

And through it all, there's this persistent, exhausting undercurrent of pressure, the pressure to handle everything without a hint of struggle, to stay endlessly grateful when you're running on vapors, to be the unshakable rock for everyone around you, and to somehow make it all look effortless even when your soul feels stretched thin.

But here's the truth you need to hear, the one you deserve to believe: ***You don't have to justify your exhaustion.***

You don't need someone's permission to admit, "This is unbelievably hard." You don't have to earn the right to rest by pushing yourself to the edge. You don't have to be everything to everyone before you're allowed to breathe.

And you definitely don't need to carry guilt for being human.

The invisible load you bear is real. The emotional weight is heavy. And feeling it, feeling overwhelmed, tired, and sometimes broken, does not mean you are weak.

It means you are carrying more than most will ever understand, and you're still standing.

You're Not Meant to Carry It All Alone

Part of what makes the invisible load so unbearably heavy is the loneliness that comes with it. There's no one stepping in to say, "Hey, let me handle this tonight." No one who finishes your sentence when you're too tired to find the words. No one who looks at you and simply knows, without being asked, that you need a break. It's all on you, every meal, every meltdown, every midnight worry.

And after a while, maybe you stopped asking for help. Maybe you've watched the people around you misunderstand your needs, minimize your exhaustion, or simply disappear when things got hard. Maybe you learned, through too many disappointments, that it's safer to rely on yourself than to hope someone else will lighten the load.

So you silently do it all. You carry it, the schedules, the worries, the broken dreams and the stubborn hope, alone. But every day you do it without support, a tiny piece of you feels chipped away, a small weariness settles deeper into your bones.

And it doesn't mean you're weak. It means you've been strong for longer than anyone should ever have to be.

Here's the truth you may have forgotten while you were busy holding up the sky:

You were never meant to carry life alone.

You weren't built to mother, heal, work, plan, nurture, and survive the impossible without someone beside you.

Needing help doesn't make you weak. It makes you human. Wonderfully, courageously human.

What you've been doing every single day, carrying the emotional weight of your family, navigating meltdown after meltdown, loving fiercely through exhaustion and loneliness, is nothing short of heroic.

But even heroes, the real ones, the messy, beautiful, exhausted ones, need someone to help carry the cape sometimes.

Even heroes deserve to be seen, supported, and allowed to rest.

This chapter isn't going to give you a five-step plan to magically make the load disappear. That wouldn't be honest. What it will do is help you take inventory, so you can see what you're carrying, identify what can be shared, and slowly start to rebuild a life that includes *you* in it.

Guided Exercise: My Load Audit

Let's take a real, honest look at everything you're carrying. Not just the tasks, but the mental and emotional weight.

Get a journal, or open a note on your phone. Draw three columns. Label them: **Mental Load**, **Emotional Load**, and **Physical Tasks**.

Now list everything that comes to mind.

Mental Load (Examples):

- Remembering appointments

- Planning meals

- Managing school schedules

- Monitoring behavior changes in your kids

- Budget tracking

Emotional Load (Examples):

- Worrying about your child's future

- Guilt about not doing "enough"

- Feeling isolated or misunderstood

- Missing your old self

- Suppressing emotions for the sake of your kids

Physical Tasks (Examples):

- Laundry

- Grocery shopping

- Cleaning the house

- Driving to school and activities

- Handling bedtime routines

Once it's all out on paper, just sit with it.

Take it in, not with judgment, but with awe.

Look at what you've been holding. Look at what you've survived. Look at the strength it takes to do this every day.

Now, take a deep breath. Circle three items that feel the *heaviest*. These are your first focus areas in the chapters ahead. You don't need to fix everything at once. Just start with three.

You weren't meant to be invisible. Neither is your load.

You're not asking for too much when you ask for rest, or help, or to be seen.

You're asking for what you've already earned.

Let's keep going.

Chapter 4

Feeling It All Without Falling Apart

There's a quiet, almost invisible moment that happens between saying "I'm fine" and feeling like you might break open. It sneaks up while you're folding tiny socks, rinsing a coffee mug, mindlessly scrolling through your phone in the five minutes you finally have to yourself. And then, without warning, the emotion rises, like a wave you didn't see coming, gripping your throat, blurring your vision, tightening your chest just enough to make you catch your breath.

But instead of letting it out, you tuck it away.

Because the kids are in the next room and need you to be okay.

Because there's homework to check and dishes to finish and lunches to pack.

Because you're terrified that if you let even one tear fall, the floodgates might open and you won't be able to pull yourself back together in time.

This is the impossible space you live in: carrying a heart full of tenderness and exhaustion while living in a world that demands you keep marching forward, no matter how heavy it gets. You have learned to be strong, but somewhere along the way, "strong" got twisted into "silent."

And here's the truth: your emotions aren't a weakness to hide or control. Feeling deeply doesn't mean you're falling apart. It means you're still beautifully, fiercely **human.**

You are allowed to feel everything, even the messy, overwhelming parts, without apology.

You Are Not "Too Much"

One of the cruelest lies women, especially single mothers, have been fed is that our emotions make us unstable. That crying means weakness. That needing a minute, or a night, or a break is some kind of failure. That we should be grateful to have children, so what right do we have to feel sad, or angry, or overwhelmed?

Let's undo that right now.

You are not too emotional.

You are not dramatic.

You are not ungrateful.

You are **human.**

You're carrying layers of experience, some joyful, some heart-breaking. You're trying to make sense of what you've lost while holding steady for the people who need you most. That kind of balancing act takes more courage than pretending you're okay ever will.

Emotional Strength Is Not Emotional Suppression

Somewhere along the way, strength became synonymous with silence. But real emotional strength isn't about holding everything in. It's about being able to sit with your feelings long enough to understand them, and still choose to keep going.

It's not the absence of emotion that makes you powerful. It's the willingness to feel it *and* keep showing up for yourself.

You're allowed to have nights when everything feels like too much.

You're allowed to be angry that you're doing this alone.

You're allowed to mourn the version of your life you thought you'd have.

You're allowed to feel joy again, even if not everything is "fixed."

The full spectrum of your emotions deserves space, not shame.

You Don't Have to Protect Everyone from Your Feelings

A lot of moms think they have to hide their emotions to protect their children. And yes, it's important to create a sense of stability, but **stability doesn't require emotional perfection.** What your kids really need is a mother who shows them that it's okay to feel, and that feelings can be felt without fear.

Let them see you process disappointment and still get back up. Let them see you cry and still keep going. That's not weakness, that's emotional fluency.

What you're modeling isn't instability, it's resilience with truth. And in a world that too often teaches kids to hide, suppress, or escape their emotions, that is a gift.

Create Space to Feel, Safely

Your feelings have been asking to be heard. And when we don't give them space, they find ways to leak out; through fatigue, irritability, anxiety, or numbness. So here's the invitation:

Let them speak. But do it in ways that feel safe.

That might look like:

- Crying in the car with music that understands you.

- Taking a walk and letting your thoughts roam freely.

- Writing in a journal with no filter or pressure to be wise.

- Talking to a therapist, a friend, or a voice note to yourself.

You don't need a perfect setup or an hour of silence. You just need a window of honesty. Even five minutes of truth can release pressure you've held for weeks.

Emotional Practice: Permission to Feel

Sometimes, the hardest part isn't the emotion itself, it's the belief that you *shouldn't* feel it. So let's shift that.

Write the following sentence at the top of a journal page or in a note on your phone:

"Today, I give myself permission to feel..."

Then, complete the sentence with whatever comes up. Don't edit. Don't justify. Just let it out.

Maybe it looks like:

- *Today, I give myself permission to feel tired without guilt.*

- *Today, I give myself permission to feel sad about what I lost.*

- *Today, I give myself permission to feel proud of how far I've come.*

Write as many sentences as you need. Read them out loud. Let them be true.

Your Feelings Are Not the Problem

Let this be the reminder you didn't even realize your heart was craving: **Your emotions are not proof that you're failing**, they are proof that you are human, still fighting, still alive inside it all. They are not flaws to fix; they are messages from your soul asking to be heard.

You're not falling apart. You're releasing years of pressure you've been carrying quietly, bravely, without a finish line in sight.

You're not weak. You're courageous enough to tell the truth about how heavy it's been.

You're not broken. You are a woman feeling every sharp, soft, overwhelming piece of life, and still finding a way to carry on with grace, even when no one else sees the cost.

That's not just resilience. That's power.

Let's keep going.

Chapter 5
The Guilt Trap

There's a voice that follows you through your day. It doesn't yell. It whispers.

"You snapped at them again."

"You forgot to send that form back."

"You're not doing enough."

"You should be grateful."

"You should be better."

That voice? That's guilt. And if you're anything like most single mothers, guilt has become an unwanted companion, one that's been sitting in your passenger seat since the moment everything changed.

Guilt is quiet but relentless. It creeps in the moment you dare to rest. It speaks up when you spend money on yourself. It shows up when you're happy, whispering that you shouldn't be. It steals moments that could be peaceful. It makes you feel like even when you're doing your best, it's still not enough.

But here's the truth: **Guilt is not always your conscience, it's often your conditioning.**

And it's time we talked about it.

Guilt Has Many Faces

Guilt doesn't always show up shouting, "I feel bad." Sometimes it slips in quietly, threading itself through the cracks of your day in ways you barely notice.

It's the voice that makes you second-guess every parenting choice, wondering if you're doing enough.

It's the whisper that calls you selfish for craving a few minutes alone with your own thoughts.

It's the invisible measuring stick that demands perfection, even when you're running on empty.

It's the pressure to downplay your own needs because "the kids come first," even if it means losing pieces of yourself.

It's the automatic apologies, for the mess, for the delay, for simply existing in a way that isn't effortless.

Guilt can weave itself into almost everything:

You might feel guilty for not giving your kids the "perfect" family you once dreamed about.

For feeling drained when all you want is to be fully present.

For missing a school performance because you had to keep the paycheck coming.

For wishing, even just for a moment, that you had time to breathe, to dream, to remember who you are outside of being "Mom."

For feeling anger, for feeling sadness, for feeling, period.

If this sounds familiar, please hear this: you are not alone. The weight of guilt is so common among single mothers it can start to feel like part of your skin, something you stop questioning because it's always there.

But guilt is not love.

And guilt is not responsibility.

You can love your children fiercely and still need space to heal. You can carry the weight of your family with grace and still honor your own heart. You are allowed to be human without apology.

Where the Guilt Comes From

Let's pull the curtain back on where this guilt really begins.

It's not born from truth. It's born from **expectation.**

The world has a long history of holding mothers to superhuman standards. And for single mothers? The bar isn't just higher, it's rigged. You're expected to:

- Be both parents.

- Provide everything financially.

- Be emotionally available at all times.

- Never complain.

- Never make mistakes.

- And do it all with grace.

When those expectations clash with your actual, very human limits, guilt rushes in to fill the gap.

But that gap? That's not a moral failure.

That's **life.**

You are not meant to meet every need, anticipate every outcome, and remain unshaken. You are not supposed to parent like you have support when you don't. You're doing something incredibly difficult, and the guilt that comes from not doing it "perfectly" is not evidence of failure. It's a signal that the expectations were never fair to begin with.

Guilt vs. Shame

Let's draw an important line.

- **Guilt** says: *"I did something wrong."*

- **Shame** says: *"I am something wrong."*

You may carry both.

Guilt when you feel like you haven't done enough.
Shame when you start to believe that *you* aren't enough.

Shame is heavier. It lingers deeper. But it thrives in silence. And silence is exactly what this chapter is here to break.

You are not a bad mother.
You are not failing.
You are not behind.
You are not selfish for wanting more.
You are not broken because you sometimes feel like walking away.

You are a woman with a full heart and a limited bandwidth, and that does not make you wrong. It makes you **real**.

Releasing the Guilt That Doesn't Belong to You

Let's say something radical: **You are allowed to let go of guilt that was never yours to carry.**

The guilt of not being able to do it all? That belongs to a society that was never designed to support you.

The guilt of not being a perfect parent? That belongs to the myth of perfection, not to your reality.

The guilt of wanting space, rest, joy, or romance? That guilt is not truth, it's control.

Start asking yourself:

- *Is this guilt helpful?*

- *Is this guilt even true?*

- *Did I actually do something wrong, or am I just overwhelmed and human?*

Some guilt is useful, it teaches, it guides. But most of what you're carrying? It's clutter. It's pressure. It's lies dressed up as duty.

You can drop it.

You Deserve Grace, Too

You give your kids grace. You forgive their bad moods, their meltdowns, their mistakes. You understand when they're tired, or scared, or not their best selves.

Now do the same for you.

The next time guilt creeps in, pause and say:

"I am doing my best. And that is allowed to be enough today."

Repeat it as many times as you need. Write it on a sticky note. Put it on your mirror. Tattoo it on your soul.

You don't need to suffer to prove you're a good mom.

You don't need to punish yourself for being human.

You are allowed to feel joy, make mistakes, grow slowly, and still be exactly what your children need.

You are allowed to be proud of how far you've come, even if no one claps.

You don't have to carry guilt like a shadow. You can stand in the light of your own truth:

You love your children deeply. You show up. You keep going. You are enough.

Let's keep going.

Chapter 6
The Inner Voice Makeover

If you spoke to your best friend the way you speak to yourself, with that sharp, relentless judgment, would she stay?

Would she trust you?

Would she feel safe, encouraged, understood?

Or would she start to shrink under the weight of criticism, self-doubt, and that edge in your tone that cuts without meaning to?

The truth is, most of us would never speak to someone we love the way we speak to ourselves.

And yet, there's that quiet voice inside. The one that loops through your mind like a broken record:

"You're not doing enough."

"You're falling behind."

"You're messing everything up."

It's quiet. It's relentless. And because it's been there so long, it feels familiar, almost normal.

But just because it's familiar doesn't mean it's true.

That voice that criticizes you isn't your intuition trying to guide you. It isn't the sound of your inner strength calling you higher. It's not the voice of your wisdom, and it certainly isn't a reflection of your worth.

It's your fear.

It's old programming, outdated, inherited stories written by exhaustion, judgment, and impossible expectations.

They are stories you took on without even realizing it, because no one ever paused to ask if they truly belonged to you, or if you were simply taught to believe they did.

And maybe now... it's time for a rewrite.

Maybe it's time to give yourself the same compassion, encouragement, and fierce love you offer so freely to everyone else.

Because you are worth speaking to, and about, with kindness.

The Voice That Follows You

Your inner voice narrates your life. It interprets your choices. It colors your days. And when you're parenting alone, especially under stress, that voice gets louder, because there's no one else in the room to balance it out.

You may have heard it just this week:

- *"Why can't you keep it together?"*

- *"You're such a mess."*

- *"Everyone else is doing better than you."*

- *"You're going to ruin your kids."*

- *"If you were stronger, this wouldn't feel so hard."*

Those words don't sound cruel when you've grown used to them. They sound... normal. Like "tough love." Like the price you pay for responsibility.

But let me be clear: **self-abuse is not self-discipline.**

Tearing yourself down doesn't make you better. It makes you smaller. It wears down your capacity to hope, to rest, to try.

You don't need to bully yourself into becoming a better version of you.

You need to **believe** in her.

Where the Voice Came From

That critical voice was planted somewhere. It didn't just appear.

It might be an echo from childhood, from a parent who demanded perfection or withheld approval.

It might be the voice of a partner who tore you down, left you doubting your worth.

It might be the accumulation of a culture that tells single moms they're a burden, a failure, a statistic.

Or it might just be the result of burnout, when everything hurts and your mind starts looking for someone to blame... and turns inward.

But now, as an adult woman, **you get to choose whether that voice stays.**

You get to say: *"This no longer serves me."*
You get to ask: *"What kind of voice do I want in my head when things get hard?"*
You get to build a new one, one rooted in truth, not fear.

What the New Voice Sounds Like

The voice inside you doesn't have to tear you down, it can be the one that lifts you up. It can offer you comfort when you're overwhelmed, gently remind you of your strength when you forget, and wrap you in kindness when the rest of the world feels like too much.

Here's what the new voice might sound like:

- *"This is hard, and I'm still showing up."*

- *"I made a mistake, but I am not a mistake."*

- *"I am not failing. I am figuring it out."*

- *"I'm allowed to be proud of myself today."*

- *"Even now, I am worthy of love."*

This isn't about slapping a smile over your struggles or pretending everything's okay when it isn't. It's about building a place inside yourself where you can breathe, where you can be honest, messy, real, so you're not always chasing comfort or validation from the outside world.

You Are the Narrator Now

For so long, your story has been filtered through someone else's expectations. Someone else decided who you were supposed to be, what you were worth, and what you should settle for.

But this chapter of your life? This version of you? It gets to be told in your own voice now.

A voice that sounds like:

Compassion when you're bone-deep tired.

Encouragement when you're doubting every step.

Honesty that feels like truth, not punishment.

Protection that wraps around you when you're too worn out to fight for yourself.

You deserve to hear that voice. You deserve to be that voice.

And your kids? They deserve to see a mother who doesn't just keep going; they deserve to see a mother who speaks to herself with the same tenderness, patience, and fierce love she gives so freely to them.

This Isn't About Flattery — It's About Safety

Changing your inner voice isn't about boosting your ego or becoming "super confident." It's about creating an internal space where **you feel safe to grow.**

We don't blossom when we're berated. We blossom when we are seen. Heard. Understood. Encouraged.

You're not lazy.
You're not broken.
You're not a bad mom.
You're not behind.
You're tired. You're grieving. You're doing your best.

And you deserve to hear that from yourself.

You may not always believe the kind voice at first. That's okay. Keep saying it anyway. Speak gently to yourself until it feels more natural than criticism. Until grace becomes your instinct.

You've heard the old voice long enough.

Let's keep going.

Chapter 7
Your Time, Energy, and Boundaries

There's a moment that sneaks up on you, usually somewhere around midweek, when you realize you've spent the week saying "yes" to everything and everyone, except yourself.

You've answered the work emails that never end, packed the lunches with whatever you could piece together, swept up the same messes that reappear like clockwork, scheduled the appointments that no one else remembers, paid the bills before anyone even noticed they were due, and fielded a thousand tiny questions that pull at your focus until you're too tired to think. Meanwhile, your own needs have been quietly pushed off to "maybe tomorrow" ... again.

Your time doesn't feel like yours anymore; it feels borrowed, spent on everyone else's needs and emergencies.

Your energy feels drained before your feet even touch the ground in the morning.

And your boundaries? If they exist at all, they feel like they're made of tissue paper, easy to tear, impossible to hold.

But what if the real act of bravery isn't about doing more or trying harder?

What if the real **revolution** is about protecting what's already yours, your time, your energy, your heart, and just letting yourself be a priority without guilt?

You Are the Resource

Let's name the truth: you are the engine of your household. The emotional anchor. The decision maker. The planner. The default parent. The one who keeps things moving, even when you're falling apart quietly inside.

And like any resource, **you are finite**.

Your energy is not endless. Your patience has limits. Your day has 24 hours, and many of those are already spoken for before you even open your eyes.

The world may ask you to give endlessly, but life gets better the moment you start asking: *What do I need to protect in order to survive this season, and maybe even grow through it?*

That's where boundaries come in.

Time Is Not the Enemy—It's the Messenger

You might feel like you never have enough time. That if you could just "get it together," manage your schedule better, wake up earlier, or hustle harder, things would feel more in control.

But most of the time, it's not a time problem.

It's a **too much** problem.
It's a **trying-to-do-everything-with-no-backup** problem.
It's a **"I keep saying yes to avoid guilt"** problem.

Your time is already trying to show you what matters. Every repeated rush. Every skipped meal. Every night you collapse into bed feeling like you got nothing done; *that's not failure.* That's your life whispering, *"Something needs to change."*

Boundaries Are Not Walls—They're Doors with Locks

Somewhere along the way, the word "boundaries" started to take on a negative meaning. It began to sound harsh, cold, even selfish, as if setting limits meant you didn't care about others. But that's not the truth. Healthy boundaries aren't walls built to shut people out. They're doors you get to control, doors you can open when it feels safe and right, and close when you need to protect your peace. Boundaries are not a rejection of others; they are a deep act of love and respect for yourself.

Boundaries protect what you value.

Right now, more than ever, you need to recognize what truly matters. You need to value your mental clarity, the ability to think your own thoughts without being buried under everyone else's demands. You need to protect your emotional well-being, the part of you that feels deeply, loves fiercely, and deserves care just as much as anyone else.

You need to cherish your time with your children, not as another chore to check off, but as sacred, irreplaceable moments that will shape both their hearts and yours. You need to honor your right to rest, without guilt, without needing to justify it. And you need to embrace your right to exist without explaining yourself to anyone.

Saying "no" doesn't make you rude; it makes you someone who knows her limits.

Cancelling plans doesn't make you unreliable; it makes you someone who chooses peace over pressure.

Asking for time doesn't make you weak; it makes you courageous enough to recognize that you matter, too.

Boundaries don't push people away, they keep resentment from growing.

What Steals Your Time and Energy Most?

It's not always the big, dramatic moments that leave you feeling drained. More often, it's the small, almost invisible leaks that quietly sap your energy day after day. It's the texts you answer out of obligation when you're already overwhelmed. It's the favors you say "yes" to, even when you're silently drowning in your own responsibilities. It's the conversations that leave you feeling emotionally hungover, questioning your worth. It's the guilt that pressures you into explaining decisions that you should never have to justify. It's the endless mental loop of planning, managing, and re-checking everything, all by yourself.

Individually, these moments might not seem like much. But together, they pile up until they quietly steal your peace, your patience, and your joy.

The answer isn't to do less across the board. It's to start doing less of what drains you and more of what restores you, with no guilt, no apology, and no permission needed.

How to Reclaim Your Time and Energy

You don't need a perfect routine. You need rhythms that work with your real life. Start simple.

Ask Yourself:

- What drains me the fastest?

- What recharges me the quickest?

- What would I love to have more time for, even just 15 minutes?

- Where am I saying yes when I want to say no?

Try This:

- **Time-block your energy**, not just your tasks. Don't just plan what you'll do, plan how you want to feel.

- **Schedule yourself in**: If someone asked for a meeting, you'd block it off. So why don't you block time for your walk, your nap, your journaling?

- **Use "no," as a sentence**: Not, "I'm sorry, I wish I could, maybe next time..." Just: *"No, that doesn't work for me."*

- **Create micro-boundaries** with your kids: You love them endlessly, but they don't need access to your attention every second. It's okay to say, "I need 10 minutes to finish this before I help."

Your Kids Don't Need You to Be Constantly Available—They Need You to Be Well

Take a moment and let that sink in.

Your children don't benefit from having a mother who gives so much of herself that there's nothing left. They benefit from a mother who knows how to breathe, how to laugh, how to rest, a mother who shows them by example what it looks like to honor her own needs without guilt.

You teach them far more through your boundaries than you ever could through your burnout. Every time you say "no" when your spirit needs a break, you are teaching them it's okay to protect their own energy someday, too.

You are not lazy for needing rest. You are not failing because you feel stretched thin. You are navigating a life filled with constant demands and still finding the courage to show up day after day.

So now, ask yourself:

What part of my day needs to be mine again?

Even if it's just five stolen minutes in a day that demands everything from you, that small space still matters. Even if it's nothing more than savoring the first sip of your coffee alone, sitting in a fragile, precious silence before the day rushes back in, it matters. Even if it's closing the bathroom door, locking it unapologetically, and giving yourself one deep breath that belongs only to you, that, too, matters.

You are not selfish for needing that space. You are not weak for craving a moment of pause. You are wise enough to know that even the strongest women need room to exhale, to feel, to simply be.

Let's not wait for some imaginary "someday" when things magically calm down. Let's begin making space right now, today, for your own rhythm to return. Let's start fiercely protecting the woman who has been holding everything and everyone together, often with no one realizing just how heavy it's been.

Let's keep going.

Chapter 8

Money, Survival, and Stability

There's a kind of anxiety that doesn't have a sound. It doesn't scream. It hums, low, constant, always in the background.

You feel it when you check your account balance before swiping your card.
You feel it when an unexpected bill lands in your inbox.
You feel it when your child asks for something small and you pause, not because you don't want to say yes, but because you're doing silent math in your head.

That hum is **financial fear**, and it's exhausting.

It's not just about dollars and cents. It's about survival. It's about safety. It's about the weight of knowing it all depends on you, and no one is coming to bail you out.

Let's talk about it. Not with shame. Not with judgment. But with honesty, and power, and the understanding that you're not just managing money. You're managing a life.

You Are Not Irresponsible; You Are Under-Resourced

Let's get something straight right now: if you are struggling financially, that is **not a reflection of your worth or intelligence.**

You're not lazy.
You're not broken.
You're not failing.

You are navigating a world that wasn't built to support single mothers. The systems weren't designed with you in mind. The safety nets have holes. The pressure is unrelenting. And still, you make it work. Somehow.

That's not failure. That's *resilience on a budget.*

Survival Mode Isn't a Strategy, It's a Warning Sign

You've probably lived in survival mode more than you care to admit. It's the zone where your decisions are based not on what's best, but on what's *possible.*

You choose the cheapest option, even if it costs more long-term.

You delay medical care.

You skip meals.

You stay in jobs, or relationships, that drain you because stability feels safer than risk.

But survival mode is **not a long-term financial plan.**

It's a trauma response.

It's a signal that you're out of bandwidth.

It's what happens when every choice feels like an emergency.

And here's what I need you to hear: **you don't have to live that way forever.**

You may not be able to change everything overnight, but there is always a path to more stability. And it begins with believing that **you deserve financial peace.**

Rewriting Your Relationship with Money

For many women, especially single mothers, money is not just numbers, it's emotion.

Money brings up fear, shame, longing, hope, resentment, scarcity, and even grief. Maybe you were raised to never talk about it. Maybe you were told someone else would always take care of it. Maybe someone once used it to control you.

But here you are, taking control back.

And that means rewriting the internal money story.

Ask yourself:

- What was I taught (explicitly or implicitly) about money growing up?

- Do I believe I'm capable of managing money well?

- Do I believe I'm allowed to have money and feel safe with it?

- What does financial stability look like to *me*, not what the world says it should be?

Your mindset matters. But this isn't just about vision boards and mantras. It's about **naming your truth and building from there.**

Let's Get Practical (Without the Shame)

This book isn't here to hand you the same tired advice like "just save more" or "skip your daily latte." You already know how to stretch a dollar until it screams. You already know how to prioritize needs over wants because you've been living that reality every day.

What this is really about is helping you take a clear, honest look at where you are right now. It's about helping you make peace with the numbers instead of feeling controlled by them. It's about helping you create safety and stability wherever you can, even if it's just one small step at a time.

So let's start with the basics.

Know Your "Enough" Budget.

This isn't your dream budget filled with spa days and tropical vacations. This is your survival baseline, the bare essentials you need covered to keep the lights on and food in the fridge: rent or mortgage, utilities, groceries, transportation, childcare, and minimum debt payments.

Knowing this number does more than just organize your finances. It helps you breathe a little easier. It gives you a foundation to plan from. It gives you clarity so that if you need to ask for help, you can do it with confidence instead of shame.

This is where rebuilding begins; with clarity, courage, and small, steady steps.

Track Emotion, Not Just Expenses

Every purchase you make carries an emotion with it. Sometimes it's hope. Sometimes it's fear, or guilt, or the deep craving for a little relief. Start paying attention to what you're really feeling when you click "buy" or swipe your card. There's a story behind every choice, and understanding that story can give you the power to make decisions that truly serve you, instead of just momentarily numbing what's underneath.

Next time you make a purchase, think about the following:

- Do I spend to cope? Avoid? Feel in control?

- What do I tell myself when I can't afford something?

- When I do have a little extra, do I feel peace or panic?

Money isn't just math, it's emotional. And awareness is your superpower.

Ask for Help (Even When It's Hard)

You are not weak for needing help. Whether it's food assistance, community resources, or a payment plan, you're allowed to use every tool available to support your family.

Asking for help doesn't make you a burden. It makes you *resourceful*.

You Deserve More Than "Just Getting By"

You're surviving. You're doing what needs to be done, pushing through the hard days, carrying it all because you have to.

But surviving isn't the dream. It's the floor, the starting point, not the finish line.

You deserve more.

You deserve breathing room, space to think, to rest, to simply exist without being pulled in a hundred directions.

You deserve real choices, not just survival-mode decisions made out of urgency and fear.

You deserve rest that doesn't carry guilt with it.

You deserve joy that feels light and unburdened.

You deserve a future that feels sturdy, not fragile, a future you can step into with hope, not fear.

You may not be there yet, and that's okay. Just because it feels far away today doesn't mean it's out of reach forever.

You don't have to build everything in a day. Healing, financially, emotionally, spiritually, happens in layers. Step by step. Moment by moment. Every small move you make toward clarity and control matters.

Even reading this chapter?

That's a step.

That's courage.

That's you, choosing yourself, even if it's just a whisper for now.

Your Worth Is Not in Your Wallet

Let this sink in.

You are not your credit score.
You are not your overdue bill.
You are not your income bracket.
You are not a bad mother because money is tight.

You are a woman navigating more than most people will ever understand, doing the very best you can with the resources, strength, and heart you have. Even when you're exhausted, even when the world feels heavy, you still show up; with love, with courage, and with the relentless, stubborn hope that tomorrow can be better than today.

And believe this: it will.

Let's keep going.

Chapter 9
The Solo Parent Playbook

There's no tag team when you're a solo parent.

No one to glance at across the room when your child melts down in public, silently asking for backup.

No partner to nudge and whisper, "Can you handle this one?" when you're running low on patience.

No one to step in after a long day and say, "Go rest, I'll take bedtime tonight."

It's just you.

It's your voice soothing fears.

Your patience stretched to its edges.

Your instincts guiding you, even when you're second-guessing yourself.

Your exhaustion quietly tucked behind your smile.

You, holding the line and softening the world for your children, over and over again, without anyone there to trade off or tag in.

Solo parenting is more than just parenting. It's being the constant when everything else feels shaky.

It's being the anchor that keeps the family grounded and the wind that keeps it moving forward.

It's doing all the emotional labor, making all the hard decisions, setting all the boundaries, and offering all the comfort, day after day, even when your own reserves feel dangerously low.

And somehow, despite it all, you keep showing up.

You keep loving.

You keep believing that what you're doing matters.

Because it does.

And so do you.

And while no playbook can make it easy, this chapter is here to remind you: **You are not doing it wrong. You're just doing a two-person job with one heart.**

Discipline Without Backup

Discipline as a solo parent often feels like walking a tightrope with no safety net beneath you. There's no one waiting at the end of the day to debrief with, no one to swap glances with across the room during a meltdown and silently ask, "Was that too harsh? Should I have let that go?" Every decision, every consequence, every moment of discipline rests solely on your shoulders.

What you do have, and it's more powerful than you realize, is your gut. Your instincts, born from love, experience, and fierce protection, are more trustworthy than you give yourself credit for. They will guide you even when doubt creeps in.

Still, disciplining without backup takes a toll. You're the one who has to enforce boundaries even when you're running on fumes. You're the one who plays the "bad guy" role when you say no, without anyone else stepping in to share the weight. You're the one who misses out on being the "fun parent" because there's no one else to trade off with. And you're the one who second-guesses herself long after the kids are in bed, replaying moments and wondering if you got it right.

It's exhausting. It's lonely. And yes, it feels deeply unfair.

Because it is *unfair.*

But here's the thing: unfair doesn't mean impossible. It doesn't mean you're failing. It doesn't mean you have to be perfect to raise good, loving, resilient kids.

You don't need flawless parenting.

You just need a handful of steady, loving tools that work for your real life, the messy, beautiful, resilient life you are building every single day.

The Real Goals of Solo Parenting

Let's get this clear: your job is not to make your child's life perfect. Your job is to raise them with love, safety, and guidance, to give them a steady place to grow, not a flawless world to live in.

You can still be an amazing parent without being "fun" every second of every day. You can love them deeply without giving them everything they ask for. You can create a safe, nurturing home without keeping it spotless all the time. And you can be a wonderful role model even if you occasionally lose your temper, because being human doesn't cancel out your love.

Every single day, you are showing your children real life. You are modeling real love, the kind that holds steady even when things are messy. You are showing them real boundaries, the kind that teach them how to be safe in the world and safe with themselves.

Every time you choose connection over control, even when it would be easier to snap or shut down, you are parenting with true power, the kind that leaves a lasting imprint not just on their behavior, but on their hearts.

What to Do When You Feel Like the Villain

One of the hardest parts of solo parenting is being the only one who says "no."

You don't get to divide roles. You don't get to say, "Ask your dad." You are the rule-maker and the comforter, all in one breath.

That creates emotional whiplash.

You want to hold your child accountable *and* hold them close. You want to correct behavior without wounding the relationship.
You want to enforce limits without feeling like the enemy.

Here's what helps:

- **Name what's happening.** Say, "I know you're upset, and I understand. But my job is to keep you safe and help you grow. That means I have to make hard choices sometimes."

- **Let yourself decompress.** After you hold a hard boundary, breathe. Shake it off. Forgive yourself for how it looked.

- **Remind yourself it's okay to be the strong one.**
  Your child may push against you, but deep down, they
  feel more secure knowing the boundary exists.

Being the "bad guy" in the moment doesn't mean you're a
bad mom. It means you're doing the work of building trust
long-term.

When Your Kids Don't See Your Sacrifices

You don't do it for the praise. But there are nights when it would
mean the world to hear, "Thanks for dinner," or "I know this is
hard for you too."

And sometimes, it stings that they don't see it.

They don't see the juggling act.
They don't see the tears behind the locked bathroom door.
They don't know that you chose groceries over new shoes again.
They just know that you're there, and they assume you always
will be.

That's part of the job. And it's one of the loneliest parts.

But what they *will* see later, is a mother who showed up. Who
didn't quit. Who stayed when staying was hard. Who didn't
have it all together, but had enough love to keep trying.

They may not say it now.
But you are writing the kind of legacy they'll carry for life.

Communication in the Solo Household

Without another adult in the home, communication with your kids becomes even more important. It's how you build trust, connection, and understanding in the middle of chaos.

A few things that work:

- **Use "we," language.** Instead of "Because I said so," try "We're a team, and here's what our family needs right now."

- **Give small choices when possible.** Kids feel empowered when they get to choose between two options you're already okay with.

- **Say what you mean and mean what you say.** Consistency creates safety. They'll push boundaries, but deep down, they want to know where the fence is.

And if you lose your cool? Apologize. Not because you "owe" them perfection, but because modeling repair is part of raising emotionally healthy humans.

You Are Enough. Yes, You.

You might question yourself daily. You might wish for someone to share the weight. You might long for a voice that says, "You're doing a great job."

So here it is:

You're doing a great job.

You are not failing because you feel overwhelmed.
You are not broken because you're tired of being strong.
You are not less than because your child doesn't have two parents in the home.

You are doing something extraordinary, parenting with your whole heart and half the support.

That's not something to hide.

That's something to be *incredibly* proud of.

Let's keep going.

Chapter 10

Rediscovering YOU

B efore the diapers.
Before the schedules and the school drop-offs.
Before the court dates, and budgeting spreadsheets, and nights you cried into your pillow, wondering how you were going to do this alone...

There was you.

Not the mother. Not the fixer. Not the planner or provider.
Just *you*.

Maybe she danced in the kitchen when no one was watching.
Maybe she lost hours in books or music or sketching or dreaming.
Maybe she said "yes" to adventure before she learned to always calculate risk.

And maybe you haven't heard her voice in a while.

This chapter is about reconnecting with the woman who still lives under the titles and the tasks. Not by escaping motherhood, but by remembering that **you were someone before all of this, and that someone still matters.**

You Are Not Just "Mom"

It happens slowly.

You give a little more. You say "not now" to yourself a little more often. You fold pieces of your personality into drawers, promising to take them out again later.

But later doesn't come.
The needs never stop.
And eventually, you start to believe that your whole identity is wrapped around who you are *to other people.*

But you are not just "Mom." You never were.

Motherhood is powerful, but it was never meant to erase you.

It's time to call yourself back.

You Deserve to Exist Outside of Service

You are more than the meals you prepare, the homework you help with, and the bills you manage.
You are more than how well you hold everything together when life feels like it's pulling you apart.

You are a woman with a full heart, vibrant dreams, quiet hopes, and a story that belongs to you, not just a chapter in someone else's life, but a beautiful, unfinished story of your own.

And that story?
It's not over.
It hasn't been shelved, forgotten, or expired.
It's still unfolding, still waiting for you to step back into it with your whole radiant self.

You are allowed to want something just for yourself, without explanation.
You are allowed to take time that isn't "productive" by anyone else's standards.
You are allowed to remember what made you feel alive before life taught you to be exhausted.

You are allowed to matter, *not just as a mother, but as a whole, worthy, breathtakingly human woman.*

"But I Don't Even Know Who I Am Anymore..."

You're not alone in that feeling. Many mothers, especially single mothers, lose sight of who they are outside the roles they've had to step into.

Here's the good news: **you don't have to rebuild yourself from scratch.**
You already exist beneath the surface.

Sometimes it's just about asking the right questions.

Ask Yourself...

- *What did I love before my life became about survival?*

- *What did I do when I didn't need it to be useful, productive, or praised?*

- *What did I stop doing because there was no time, no support, or no room?*

- *When was the last time I felt like me?*

You don't have to go back to everything. But if one tiny ember still glows under the ash of this season, you can start there.

You don't need a full makeover. You need a homecoming.

The Lie of "When Things Calm Down..."

You've probably told yourself: *When the kids are older... when work slows down... when I have more money...*
Then I'll focus on myself again.

But the truth is, life rarely just "calms down." It shifts. It rearranges. It throws new things at you when you're least ready.

Waiting for the perfect time to reconnect with yourself is like waiting for silence in a crowded room. You might be waiting forever.

Instead, what if you started with 15 minutes a week?
What if you gave yourself a small yes?

You don't need hours. You need *permission*.

Let Her Out

Put on the playlist you loved when you were 23.
Buy the sketchpad, the lipstick, the thrifted earrings that say "remember me?"
Text the friend who makes you feel human again.
Take yourself on a walk with no destination.
Write a journal entry that doesn't have to be deep, just honest.

Your identity isn't gone. It's just buried under survival. And now? You're choosing to dig.

When You Reconnect with You, Everything Changes

When you remember who you are, it shifts your parenting.
Your patience deepens. Your presence sharpens. Your exhaustion starts to make sense.
Not because you magically have more energy, but because you're no longer pouring from an identity crisis.

Your kids benefit when you're more, *you*.

Not a perfect you.
Not a version of you who never struggles.
But a grounded, centered, honest you, who knows who she is,
even if no one else is watching.

You don't have to abandon yourself to love your children.
You can love them more fully when you include yourself in that
love.

This is not the end of your story. It's a chapter of return.

Let's keep going.

Chapter 11
Love After Loss or Letdown

Y ou want to believe it's still possible, that real love, the kind that feels like peace and not performance, still exists somewhere out there for you.

But it's more complicated now.

You've seen too much to believe blindly.
You've felt heartbreak in ways you can't always put into words.
You've been disappointed more times than you'd ever admit out loud.

Maybe you opened up, shared your truth with someone you trusted, only to be ghosted when you needed connection the most.
Maybe you stayed too long in a place that made you feel small, unseen, and tired of fighting for scraps of love.
Maybe you poured every part of yourself into someone who was never truly capable of holding it, no matter how much you gave.

And now, deep down, you wonder:

Can I trust again?

Will anyone see me as more than just a mom?

Is there still room in my life, and my heart, for love that feels safe, mutual, and real?

The answer, though soft and trembling at first, is yes.

Yes, you can trust again, slowly, carefully, and on your own terms.

Yes, real love, the healing kind, can find you.

Yes, you are still desirable. You are still worthy. You are still allowed to want more than just survival.

You are allowed to want love, not because you need someone to fix you, but because you deserve to be fully seen, fully valued, and deeply loved — just as you are.

But let's start with this: **you don't need to be healed to be loved.**

Grief Wears Many Outfits

Love after loss doesn't always begin with a spark. Sometimes it begins with a sigh.

You sigh when you see a happy couple at the park and feel that strange twist in your chest.

You sigh when you realize it's been months since anyone asked you how *you're* doing.

You sigh when you climb into bed alone again, and the ache of touch you're not receiving rises to the surface.

That sigh is grief.

Grief for the love that ended.

Grief for the version of your life you thought you'd have.

Grief for the parts of yourself you gave away too easily, or held back out of fear.

You are allowed to grieve. Even if it's been years. Even if you chose to leave. Even if you thought you were over it.

Grief is not a weakness. It's a sacred goodbye.

Redefining Love: This Time, It's For You Too

You've probably spent years being told that love means sacrifice, that real relationships are supposed to be hard, that if you just give enough, love will come back around. You learned to pour yourself out, to stretch yourself thin, hoping it would be enough to make someone stay.

But now?

Now you get to redefine love on your own terms.

This time around, love should feel safe, not suspenseful, not like you're waiting for the ground to disappear beneath you.

It should feel steady, not like a roller coaster that leaves you dizzy and second-guessing your worth.

It should feel like belonging and freedom braided together, not a gilded prison where you're afraid to grow.

This time, love should fit the real you, the you that no longer shrinks herself to fit into someone else's comfort zone.

You've lived enough life to know what you won't tolerate anymore.

And now, you have the beautiful, powerful chance to discover what you truly want, and to hold out for the kind of love that feels like home, not a battle.

You Are Not "Too Much" or "Too Late"

Let's name the lies that keep love at arm's length.

"I have too much baggage."
No, you have experiences. Wisdom. Lived reality. That's not baggage, it's depth.

"I'm too busy for love."
You're not too busy. You're just not willing to shrink your life to accommodate someone who doesn't expand it.

"No one wants a woman with kids."

The *wrong* person might not. The *right* person will see your motherhood as part of your magic.

"I don't even know how to date anymore."

You don't have to be perfect. You just have to be *you*. Honest. Open. Clear about what you deserve.

You are not behind. You are not broken. You are not hard to love.

You are simply **not available for anything less than real anymore.**

When (and If) You're Ready

There's no pressure to jump back in. You don't owe the world a romantic comeback. You're not missing a piece, you are whole, with or without a partner.

But if something inside you whispers, *"I still believe in love..."*—listen.

Readiness isn't a checklist you complete or a perfect emotional state you finally arrive at. It's quieter, deeper than that.

It looks like understanding that you don't need someone to swoop in and rescue you. You're not looking to be saved, you're looking to be truly seen for who you are.

It's knowing exactly what you bring to the table, your heart, your resilience, your hard-earned wisdom, and refusing to shrink or apologize for it.

It's having the strength to walk away from anything, or anyone, who demands that you sacrifice your peace just to keep the connection.

It's prioritizing emotional safety over surface-level sparks, because you've learned that real love isn't about chaos or confusion; it's about feeling safe to be fully yourself.

Readiness isn't about being perfectly healed. It's about showing up honestly, with your scars, your growth, your messy middle, and allowing someone new to meet you there, without pretending to be anything you're not.

Dating With Children

Dating as a mother isn't just about finding someone who makes you laugh or shares your interests. It's about protecting your time, your energy, and the sacred space you've built for your family. Your heart is more guarded now, not out of fear, but out of wisdom, hard-earned through everything you've survived.

That's exactly why your standards should be sky high, without apology.

Anyone who wants to be part of your life must respect your time and the lives of your children. They must see your kids not as baggage, but as the very reason you move through life with such fierce love and determination. They must be consistent in their actions, clear in their communication, and emotionally available in ways that don't make you question your own worth.

Most importantly, they must bring peace into your world, not pressure, not chaos, and not confusion.

You are not asking for too much. You are asking for what is right, for what has always been right, and for what you and your children absolutely deserve.

The Real Love Story

The real love story doesn't begin when someone new falls for you.

It begins when *you* fall for yourself again.

When you look in the mirror and no longer see someone abandoned, but someone **becoming.**
When you stop shrinking or settling.
When you choose softness again, even after what tried to harden you.
When you say: "I am lovable exactly as I am, right here, in this chapter."

Whether or not someone else is by your side, that is love. That is worth. That is enough.

And if love comes again? Let it come gently. Let it come slow. Let it come with the same reverence you now give yourself.

You don't need to rush.
You don't need to prove.
You don't need to beg for what should show up on its own.

Love will meet you where you are, especially once you've come home to yourself.

Let's keep going.

Chapter 12
Health, Rest, and Joy Are Not Optional

You've skipped meals without thinking twice, skipped sleep more nights than you can count, and skipped silence because there's never enough time for stillness.

You've powered through headaches that throbbed behind your eyes, cramps that bent you over, back pain that made standing feel like a chore, and brain fog that made even minor tasks feel overwhelming.

You've put off check-ups you know you needed, cancelled appointments you promised yourself you'd reschedule, and ignored warning signs your body was pleading for you to notice.

Because there's always something more urgent, a child who needs help with homework, a bill that has to be paid, a pile of responsibilities that won't handle themselves.

Because someone always needs something, and you've taught yourself to come last.

Because somewhere along the way, rest started to feel like a luxury you had to earn instead of a basic need you deserved.

But beneath all of that noise, there's a quiet truth you can't silence forever: **You are not a machine.** You are not built to run on empty.

Your body is not some tool to be pushed until it breaks.

Your health is not an afterthought, not a footnote at the end of everyone else's needs.

Your joy isn't optional, it's essential.

These things are not extra. They are the foundation. And if you don't tend to them, if you keep putting yourself last, everything else you're trying so hard to hold together will start to unravel, thread by thread.

You've Been in Survival Mode for So Long, It Feels Normal

When you're a single mom, survival mode doesn't feel like a temporary season, it slowly becomes a way of life. It becomes second nature to move through your days on autopilot, pushing forward even when your body and mind are waving red flags.

You've learned how to function while sleep-deprived, waking up after restless nights and pouring coffee over exhaustion you can't shake. You've carried the weight of constant stress, juggling a hundred invisible responsibilities that never seem to shrink. You've gone nutritionally depleted, grabbing bites of whatever is left on your child's plate instead of feeding yourself first. You've navigated emotional overwhelm, burying your own feelings under the mountain of everyone else's needs. You've been physically exhausted from constant demands on your time, energy, and even your personal space, worn-down, stretched thin in every way a human can stretch.

But just because you've learned to survive this way doesn't mean you're meant to stay here. You deserve more than survival. You deserve to live, to breathe, to thrive, not just to make it through.

Because here's what survival mode never tells you:
You can function and still be fading.

And sooner or later, your body and soul will send the invoice.

Burnout. Breakdowns. Bitterness.
They don't come out of nowhere, they're signals from a self who's been neglected for too long.

You deserve better than collapse. You deserve care.

Rest Is Not a Reward

It's time to tear down the lie that says you have to earn rest, that somehow you need to work yourself to the bone before you're allowed to take a breath. Rest is not for the lazy. Rest is not selfish. Rest is not some prize you win after finishing an endless to-do list.

Rest is your birthright.

It's your reset button, the way your body, mind, and spirit recover enough to keep moving forward. Without it, everything starts to crumble, no matter how hard you try to push through.

You don't need to justify rest. You don't need to explain why you need a break. You simply need to protect it, fiercely, un-apologetically.

And it doesn't have to start with anything grand. Begin with something small and doable: Go to bed earlier one night this week, even if the laundry isn't folded. Take a nap without feeling guilty for the dishes in the sink. Sit down while your child watches a show and let yourself truly rest without the hum of shame in your mind. Close your eyes for five full minutes and breathe deeply, just for you.

This is not weakness. This is wisdom. This is how strong women stay strong, by refusing to let themselves be depleted into dust.

You Don't Have to "Get Fit"—You Have to Get Present

Let's talk about health, but not the Pinterest version. Not the "30-day transformation" plans that promise perfection. Not the green smoothie hustle or the endless pressure to "bounce back" overnight.

Let's talk about the kind of health that actually matters, the kind that whispers:

I want to feel strong enough to lift my child without strain. I want the energy to enjoy my afternoons instead of crawling toward bedtime. I want to wake up without aches that make the day feel harder than it needs to be. I want to be here, truly here, for my kids, for my dreams, for myself, for many years to come.

This kind of health isn't about perfection. It's about movement that feels good in your body, whether that's a walk around the block, stretching in the living room, or dancing in the kitchen.

It's about food that nourishes you, foods that give you real energy, real strength, not guilt or shame.

It's about deep, guilt-free rest, rest that rebuilds your mind, your muscles, and your spirit.

And most importantly, it's about learning to listen to your body's needs with compassion, not punishment. It's about

honoring the body that has carried you through every single
hard day and giving it the care it deserves.

What Joy Looks Like in Real Life

Joy doesn't always arrive with fireworks or extravagant vacations. Sometimes, joy is found in the small, quiet moments that
stitch your life together in beautiful, ordinary ways.

It's in eating a warm meal without rushing, allowing yourself
to savor every bite. It's dancing barefoot in your kitchen to the
song that never fails to wake up something alive inside you. It's
curling up with a book and reading a chapter just because you
want to, not because you have to. It's laughing out loud at a
silly show while you sit alone on the couch, letting the laughter
roll through you without apology. It's hearing your child belly
laugh across the room and feeling your heart swell with the quiet
realization: I created that moment.

You don't have to wait for the "right" time to feel good again. Joy
doesn't require permission. It doesn't wait for your bills to be
paid or your house to be spotless. It doesn't ask if you've checked
everything off your endless to-do list.

Joy is not something extra to sprinkle on top of a "perfect"
life. Joy is essential, a life-giving, soul-anchoring necessity that
belongs to you right now, exactly as you are.

Making Space Without Making It Perfect

You might be thinking that you don't have time for any of this. Maybe you're telling yourself, "I'll rest later, after things calm down," or feeling like it's indulgent to even consider putting yourself first when there's so much to do.

I want to gently say: No more waiting.

You don't need an entire day at the spa to begin reclaiming your energy. Sometimes, all you need is a 10-minute walk outside, a few deep breaths of fresh air filling your lungs.

You don't need a perfect, magazine-cover diet. You need food that sustains you, meals that don't leave you crashing halfway through the afternoon.

You don't need three uninterrupted hours of silence (though wouldn't that be lovely?). You need just ten minutes where no one calls your name, where you can hear your own thoughts again.

This isn't an all-or-nothing journey. It's made of small, consistent acts of reclamation, choosing yourself in small ways, over and over, until choosing yourself feels natural, not guilty.

You matter.

Your body matters.

Your peace matters.

And you deserve to make space for all of it, starting exactly where you are.

You Are Not a Martyr—You Are a Mother, and You Matter

No one benefits when you run yourself into the ground.

Your children don't need a burnt-out version of you.
They need a mom who laughs again.
Who breathes again.
Who treats herself like someone worth taking care of.

You are. You always have been.

So here's your permission slip:

- You can go to sleep early.

- You can say "not tonight" and mean it.

- You can do nothing and let that be enough.

- You can feed your body like it deserves to be loved.

- You can chase joy, not just survival.

This is your reminder: **You are not optional.**

Let's keep going.

Chapter 13
Finding Your People

There's a unique kind of loneliness that doesn't come from being alone.

It comes from being surrounded by people, but still feeling unseen.

It comes from doing everything for everyone, but feeling like no one would notice if you disappeared.

It comes from giving until you're empty, and realizing there's no one pouring back into you.

Single motherhood can be isolating in ways no one prepares you for.

Not because you aren't capable. But because we were never meant to carry life alone.

You weren't designed to hold everything by yourself.

You weren't meant to raise children, build stability, grieve loss, manage emotions, and maintain a home, without someone there to say, *"You don't have to do it all. I've got you."*

You need people. Not just warm bodies in your space, but safe people. Supportive people. Real people.

Let's talk about how to find them, and what to do if you've forgotten what that even looks like.

What Real Support Feels Like

Support isn't just a polite text that says, "Let me know if you need anything." Real support is deeper, messier, and far more powerful.

It's someone showing up with a hot meal when you're too tired to even think about dinner. It's someone who sees through your brave smile and your "I'm fine," and chooses to sit with you anyway, without needing you to explain.

It's someone who listens to the things you're afraid to say out loud, who helps without keeping a silent tally of favors owed, who reminds you, gently, fiercely, that you don't have to be perfect to deserve love.

Support looks like practical help when you're in a bind, and emotional validation when you're overwhelmed. It's about presence, not always solutions. Just someone being there, steady and quiet, reminding you that you are not alone.

You don't need a crowd cheering for you from a distance. You need a circle, a few trusted souls who step into the hard places with you and stay.

If You've Been Burned Before

Maybe you've opened your heart before, only to be met with silence when you needed understanding the most. Maybe you trusted someone, invited them into your world, and they didn't stay. Maybe the very people who were supposed to protect and support you were the ones who hurt you the most.

So now, you hesitate. You build walls, not because you don't crave connection, but because the risk of being let down again feels too heavy to bear.

You tell yourself it's safer not to need anyone. You convince yourself you can't afford the vulnerability.

And you know what? That makes sense. That's human. That's survival.

But there's a difference between protecting your heart and completely closing it off. Your heart might need some armor after everything it's endured, but it still needs connection just as much as it needs protection.

Healing doesn't demand giant leaps. It starts with small, careful steps, opening yourself up, just a little at a time, to the possibility that safe, steady love still exists.

You are still worthy of the kind of love you don't have to chase, the kind that meets you exactly where you are.

Where to Look (and What to Look For)

You don't have to wait for the "right" person to come knocking on your door. You can *begin* building your support system, piece by piece, moment by moment.

Here's where to begin looking:

- **Other single moms.** No one gets it like someone living it. Even one honest conversation can change your entire week.

- **Online support groups.** Look for communities that feel safe, not performative. Places where people talk real and lift each other up.

- **School connections.** If your child is in daycare or school, another mom at pickup may be just as hungry for connection as you are.

- **Local nonprofits or churches.** Many host parent groups, support circles, or events where you don't have to explain your life to be included.

- **Therapists or support professionals.** Emotional safety sometimes starts with one person trained to hold your story with care.

And when you're ready, when your spirit nudges you, *be brave enough to reach first.*

Sometimes your people are just waiting for permission to step closer.

What to Say When You Need Help

One of the hardest things to do is ask for help, especially when you're used to doing it all. For so long, you've been the one everyone leans on, the fixer, the planner, the steady hand in the chaos. But here's the truth you might need to hear again: asking for help isn't weakness. It's strength in its most honest, courageous form.

Sometimes asking for help looks like saying, "I don't need advice; I just need someone to listen for five minutes." Other times, it's reaching out and saying, "Could you come sit with me for a bit? I don't want to be alone tonight." It might even be admitting, "I'm drowning this week. Could you pick up the kids from school?" Or, "I haven't had a real conversation in days. Want to come over and talk while I fold laundry?"

You don't have to pretend you've got it all together. You don't have to hide the parts of you that feel overwhelmed, tired, or lonely. The people who truly belong in your life won't love you less for your mess. They won't flinch at your vulnerability. They will meet you in it, sit with you in it, and remind you that you never have to carry everything alone.

Boundaries and Belonging

Support doesn't mean stretching yourself thin to say yes to everyone. It doesn't mean clinging to toxic people out of fear that being alone is somehow worse than being drained.

Real support means choosing relationships that feel mutual, not one-sided, connections where you both give and receive care, understanding, and respect. It means having the courage to say "no" to energy vampires, the people who leave you feeling emptier every time, and "yes" to those who pour life back into you without strings attached.

It means letting go of connections that only survive because of guilt, habit, or a sense of obligation that weighs you down more than it lifts you up.

You're allowed to curate your circle with intention. You're allowed to say, "I need more than this," and mean it without apology.

Because when you find your people, your real, soul-deep people, you'll know.

They'll feel like coming home.

They'll feel like exhaling after you've been holding your breath for far too long.

You Don't Have to Do Life Alone Anymore

There is someone out there who will sit beside you in the mess, not flinch when you cry, and still believe in your future.

There is someone who will say, *"I see you. I've got you. You don't have to carry this alone."*

You are not too broken to be held.
You are not too complicated to be understood.
You are not too much to be loved.

You are just right, for the right people.

And they will find you faster when you start believing you're worth finding.

Let's keep going.

Chapter 14

Raising Emotionally Resilient Kids

You've asked yourself the question more times than you can count:

Am I doing enough for them?

You look into their eyes, and you want to give them the world. You want them to feel whole, safe, seen, steady, even when life doesn't look the way you planned.

And if you're honest?
You sometimes worry that the chaos, the stress, the absence of a partner, or the heavy days might hurt them.
You carry guilt when you lose your temper, when you can't afford something, when your answers are short and your patience is thinner than usual.

But here's the truth that doesn't get said enough:

You don't have to give your children a perfect life to raise whole, grounded, emotionally resilient humans.

You just have to keep showing up, with love, with honesty, and with the willingness to grow together.

Emotional Resilience Doesn't Come From Ease

It's tempting to believe that the best thing you can give your kids is comfort. And of course, we want their lives to be soft, joyful, full of safety and warmth.

But real resilience? It comes from weathering the storm, not avoiding it.

Your kids are learning from you every single day.
They are watching how you cope.
They are absorbing how you treat yourself when things go wrong.
They are noticing how you repair after conflict, how you breathe through stress, how you cry and still carry on.

And what they see is this:

A mother who doesn't pretend everything is fine, but chooses love and truth, anyway.

That's what stays with them.

It's Not About Perfection—It's About Repair

You're going to get it wrong sometimes.

You're going to raise your voice.
You're going to snap.
You're going to be distracted, or overwhelmed, or say the wrong thing.

And that's okay.

Because what matters most isn't never making mistakes, it's what happens *after*.

Here's what builds emotional resilience in your child:

- Saying "I'm sorry" and meaning it.

- Letting them express anger or sadness without shutting them down.

- Giving them language to name what they feel.

- Showing them that conflict doesn't mean disconnection.

Every time you model emotional repair, you teach them that relationships can survive rough moments. That love is strong enough to hold real feelings. That mistakes don't mean it's over.

You teach them safety, not silence.

Help Them Feel Seen—Not Just Managed

It's easy to slip into survival mode parenting. You're balancing so much, and sometimes it feels like all you do is direct traffic.

But emotional resilience starts with a child feeling seen, not just managed.

Try this:

- Pause and make eye contact when they're speaking to you.

- Use their name when you respond.

- Reflect their feelings instead of correcting them immediately. (Example: "It makes sense that you're upset. That was disappointing.")

- Ask open-ended questions like, "What was the hardest part of your day?" or "What made you smile today?"

Small, meaningful connection moments create safety. And safety is the soil where resilience grows.

You Don't Have to Be Both Parents

Let's clear this up right now:
You don't have to compensate for who's not in the room.

You don't have to be both mother and father. You don't have to stretch yourself beyond your limits, over-perform, over-give, or try to fill a space you didn't create.

Your children are not looking for a replacement. They are looking for you, present, emotionally available, consistent, and real.

Yes, there will be moments when they feel the absence of what isn't there. That's a natural part of their story. But even more powerful is what they will feel: the steady, unwavering presence of what is.

They will remember the way you made space for their feelings, even when your own heart was heavy. They will remember the way you wrapped them in love, even when you were exhausted. They will remember the soft, safe place you created for them to land when the world outside felt sharp and overwhelming.

And that steady, loving presence you offer, day after day, moment after moment, will be more than enough.

When You Worry You're Messing Them Up

Let me say what you might need to hear most:

If you are worried about being a good mom, it means you already are one.

Emotionally resilient children aren't raised by perfect parents. They're raised by parents who keep showing up, who keep trying even on the days when it feels impossibly hard.

You are teaching your children, in a hundred small ways, that emotions are not something to hide or be ashamed of. You are showing them that being human means making mistakes, learning, and growing, not pretending to have it all figured out.

You are teaching them that love isn't fragile or conditional; it's something steady, something they can trust. You are showing them that boundaries can be set with kindness and still hold strong. And you are giving them the gift of knowing that healing is possible, even when life is messy and imperfect.

When they look back years from now, they won't remember whether the house was spotless, or the meals were homemade every night. They won't remember a mother who never stumbled. They will remember a strong, warm, beautifully human woman who kept loving them, kept believing in them, and kept showing up, even when she doubted herself.

They will remember your love. They will remember your courage. And that's what will shape them most of all.

Let's keep going.

Chapter 15
Your Legacy
Starts Now

Y ou might not realize it, but every single day, you're already building something that will outlast you.

Your legacy isn't measured in money, status updates, or polished Instagram photos. It's woven into the fabric of your ordinary moments, the ones no one else sees but matter deeply.

It lives in the quiet decisions you make when no one's watching. In the middle-of-the-night comforting when little hands reach for you in the dark. In the moments you stayed patient when it would have been easier to walk away, when you spoke softly instead of shouting, when you kept showing up even though no one was clapping or even noticing.

That's what legacy looks like, not the kind that comes with plaques or standing ovations, but the kind that's built quietly, tenderly, in real time. It's made with tired hands, an aching body, and a heart that somehow stays open, even when the world feels heavy.

And it will outlast you in all the best ways.

What Your Kids Will Remember

They won't remember if the dishes were always clean or if the laundry baskets were ever empty. They won't remember whether you hosted picture-perfect birthday parties or packed perfect little lunches with handwritten notes.

They won't remember what you wore, how immaculate the house looked, or whether every sock had a match.

But they will remember how you made them feel after a hard day, how you became their safe place when the world felt heavy.

They will remember the way your voice softened when they cried, offering comfort even when you were tired to your bones.

They will remember the smell of dinner, even if it was takeout eaten on the couch while you all laughed at the same silly movie.

They will remember the feeling of being chosen, of being prioritized, even when life was loud and chaotic.

Most of all, they will remember that you kept showing up, day after exhausting day. They will remember that you tried, that you made room for their feelings, and that somehow, impossibly, you found a way to keep going even when everything felt like it was breaking.

That's what will stay with them.

That's your legacy.

You Are Not Just Surviving—You Are Shaping

Every time you hold a boundary, you are teaching your children what self-respect looks like. Every time you offer a heartfelt apology, you are showing them how to repair relationships with honesty and humility. Every time you choose to be present rather than chasing perfection, you are helping them learn how to love themselves with grace.

You are laying emotional foundation stones every single day, whether you see it or not.

And here's the part we don't say nearly enough: you don't have to wait for some far-off "someday" to create something beautiful. You are creating it right now.

Every time you speak to yourself with kindness instead of criticism, you are building it. Every time you reclaim a piece of your identity that was put on hold, you are building it. Every time you choose rest, joy, peace, or truth, even in small ways, you are adding another strong, beautiful stone to their foundation.

You are not just raising children.

You are also raising yourself, into the woman you were always meant to become.

The Pain Doesn't Get the Final Word

Maybe your story didn't begin the way you dreamed it would. Maybe your path has been marked by heartbreak, betrayal, abandonment, or devastation that left scars you're still learning to carry.

Maybe there have been nights, more than you can count, when you questioned your worth, wondering if you were enough.

But here's what matters most: your pain does not get to write your entire story.

You do.

You are the one holding the pen now, shaping the chapters that come next.

And what you create from here can be filled with grace, grit, truth, softness, and fire. It can be layered with wisdom forged in the hard places, beauty born from resilience, and hope that refuses to be extinguished.

What you have survived becomes part of the strength you pass down to those who walk beside you.

What you have healed becomes part of the safety you offer to others, a shelter built by your own hands.

And what you reclaim, piece by powerful piece, becomes part of the freedom your children, and your future self, will feel and live into.

Let that be the legacy.

A Living Legacy

You don't have to be perfect to leave behind a beautiful legacy. You don't have to get everything right or have all the answers. What matters most is that you are honest.

Honest in the way you love, even when it's messy or tired.

Honest in the boundaries you set, even when they're hard to hold.

Honest in your humanity, showing your children that it's okay to be real, to feel, to stumble, and to begin again.

If your children grow up knowing how to sit with their feelings, how to forgive themselves and others, and how to come home to who they truly are, it's because you led them there, imperfectly, bravely, beautifully.

That's not a coincidence.

That's legacy on purpose, built day by day with love, courage, and grace.

You Are the Story They'll Tell One Day

One day, your child might sit across from someone they love and say:

"My mom was the strongest person I've ever known."
"She didn't always have it easy, but she showed up every day with heart."
"She taught me what love looks like when it's hard."

When they speak of you, it won't be because you lived a perfect life. It will be because you lived a real one.

Because you chose love, not just once, but again and again, even when it would have been easier to close off.

Because you chose growth, even when no one was watching, even when the progress felt painfully slow.

Because you never stopped trying, even when the road stretched longer than you thought you could endure and the load you carried felt impossibly heavy.

You don't have to transform into someone else to leave a lasting mark on this world.

You only have to become fully, unapologetically, and honestly yourself, the woman you were always meant to be.

Not later. Not when things get easier. Not when life feels more polished.

Right here. Right now.

Your legacy doesn't start in some distant future. It begins the very moment you believe, deep in your bones, that who you are today is already worthy of being remembered.

And you are.

Let's keep going.

Chapter 16
Defining Your New Normal

You have lived through the unraveling, the unexpected endings, the long, lonely nights. You've wiped away tears in the dark, made impossible decisions alone, and summoned strength even on days when you felt like you had none left to give.

You adapted. You survived. You kept going when everything inside you whispered it would be easier to give up.

But survival isn't the end of your story.

Now, you are ready for more. You are ready to build something new, something entirely your own, not pieced together from what was lost, not shaped by what someone else abandoned, and not confined by what society says a "good mother" should be.

This chapter of your life is about redefining what fulfillment looks like. It's about deciding that you are no longer waiting for life to return to what it once was. Instead, you are choosing to move forward into something better, something beautiful, something built with your own hands and your own heart.

You Don't Have to Go Back

Maybe the life you had before this was beautiful.
Or maybe it was painful, toxic, disconnected.

Either way, what's behind you is no longer your blueprint.

So many women waste years trying to recreate the life they once knew, or the one they were told they were supposed to want.

But here's what you get to say now:

"That version of life no longer fits me."
"That wasn't working for me."
"I'm not going back, I'm moving forward."

This is your permission to stop rebuilding ruins.

You're allowed to build new ground. Ground that feels stable. Ground that feels sacred. Ground that feels like *yours*.

What Does *Your* Normal Look Like?

Your new normal doesn't have to match anyone else's version of success or happiness.

It doesn't have to look perfectly balanced. It doesn't have to be fueled by constant hustle. It doesn't have to resemble "having it all together" in a way that fits someone else's expectations.

Maybe your new normal looks like slow Saturday mornings, staying in pajamas until nearly noon, letting your home be filled with laughter instead of rigid schedules.

Maybe it's having pizza for dinner three nights in a row and feeling no guilt because you chose connection over cooking.

Maybe it's taking a daily walk where your phone stays in your pocket and you finally get a few moments to hear your own thoughts.

Maybe it's saying no to things that drain you, even if you used to say yes out of habit or obligation.

Maybe it's having a bedtime routine that includes you, not just everyone else's needs, because you finally understand you deserve care, too.

The truth is, your new normal begins the moment you stop waiting for life to feel "right" again and start defining what "right" means for you, right here, right now.

You're Allowed to Choose Peace

Maybe your old life was chaotic.
Maybe love meant anxiety.

Maybe every day felt like walking on eggshells or chasing approval.

But now?
You are allowed to choose **peace** over pressure.
You are allowed to choose **ease** over proving something.
You are allowed to choose **presence** over perfection.

Peace doesn't mean your life is quiet or calm every moment.
It means you no longer choose chaos when calm is an option.
It means you protect your energy like it matters, because it does.

You Can Stop Trying to "Catch Up"

You're not behind.

Not because your friends bought houses.
Not because your sister got promoted.
Not because your ex moved on and posts curated photos with someone new.

You are right where you're meant to be, growing in real time, through real things.

Comparison steals the joy of your progress.

Let yourself feel proud of things that might seem small to others:

- Getting the bills paid this month.

- Not crying when you really wanted to.

- Crying when you needed to.

- Feeding yourself something warm.

- Smiling at your reflection.

- Saying "I'm okay" and meaning it for the first time in a long while.

This is what becoming looks like.

You're not catching up. You're coming home.

It's Okay to Want a Soft Life

You've carried so much for so long that softness might feel unfamiliar, even a little uncomfortable. But true strength isn't about constant pushing, proving, or enduring without pause.

Strength can also look like letting your shoulders relax at the end of a hard day. It can sound like letting your voice soften when speaking to yourself with kindness. It can feel like allowing people to help you, even when every part of you is used to handling it all alone. It can be choosing to release roles and expectations you never wanted or needed to carry in the first place.

You don't need a life that constantly tests your limits or asks you to prove your worth through struggle.

You deserve a life that makes room for breathing deeply, for savoring beauty, and for simply being, without guilt.

Your softness is not a sign of weakness. It's living, breathing proof that you are healing, that you are reclaiming space for your full humanity.

Make It Yours

Write your own rhythm.
Design a life that works for *you and your kids,* not someone else's standard.
Let your new normal reflect the woman you've become, not the girl you used to be, or the mom you thought you had to be.

This time, you get to choose:

- Who has access to you.

- What you give your time and energy to.

- What rest looks like.

- What joy feels like.

- What matters.

This is your life now, not a replica of someone else's blueprint, not a copy of what the world told you it should look like. This life is yours, forged through fire, grace, truth, and the courageous act of rebuilding.

You earned this new beginning with every hard choice, every painful lesson, every moment you kept going when you weren't sure you could.

You are living proof that starting over doesn't mean you're starting from nothing. It means you are starting from a place of deep wisdom, wisdom carved out by experience, strength, and resilience.

You are starting from clarity, the kind that only comes after the fog lifts and the dust settles.

Most importantly, you are starting from you, the truest, bravest version of yourself, ready to move forward on your own terms.

Let's keep going.

Chapter 17
The Empowered Mom Manifesto

There's a moment when you stop surviving and start standing.

Not because everything has been fixed.

Not because the pain has magically disappeared.

But because somewhere deep inside, a voice gets louder than the fear, louder than the doubt, louder than the guilt.

A voice that says:

I am still here. And I still get to live.

You didn't just endure this chapter of life; you *transformed* through it.

You cried quietly in bathrooms and still showed up for morning routines.

You had hard conversations, made impossible choices, and kept your children's hearts safe, sometimes at the cost of your own.

You lived entire lifetimes between sunrise and bedtime, carrying what most people never even see.

And through all of that, you became someone stronger than you ever thought you'd need to be.

This chapter is for **her.**

The Manifesto

I am a woman before I am a role.
I am a human being before I am a caretaker.
I am a soul with dreams, with needs, with worth, not just a body in motion.

I do not owe the world my exhaustion to prove I'm doing enough.
I will no longer apologize for needing rest, joy, love, or help.

I am not broken because I feel tired.
I am not failing because I need time.
I am not behind—I am becoming.

I release the myth of perfection.
I release the weight of shame.
I release the pressure to do it all alone.

I honor the strength it takes to hold the line.
I honor the softness it takes to stay open.
I honor the courage it takes to keep showing up.

I was never meant to disappear beneath the needs of everyone else.

I was never meant to earn love through self-sacrifice.
I was never meant to abandon myself to be "enough."

I am not just a single mother. I am a whole woman.
A full, rich, layered person who still gets to dream.
Still gets to thrive. Still gets to choose.

My story is still unfolding.
My voice is still rising.
My legacy is already being written.

And today, I choose to live, not just get through.
To feel, not just function.
To build, not just hold together.

I am not less because I'm alone.
I am more because I kept going.

This is my power.
This is my truth.
This is my beginning.

Now What?

You've made it here, you've read the words, done the hard, heart-deep work, faced your shadows, and stood bravely in your own light.

But this isn't where the journey ends.

This is the beginning of a new chapter.

It's an invitation to keep choosing yourself, not as an act of rebellion against your children, but as a commitment to them. Because when they watch you live fully, they learn that love must include the self.

It's a call to keep writing your own story, not one borrowed from old expectations, but one built by your own hands, shaped by your voice, your needs, your joy.

It's permission to step into your next season with clarity and compassion, to move forward without apology. You don't owe anyone an explanation for your healing. You only owe it to yourself to reclaim your life, and to live it, boldly and beautifully.

You Did This

You didn't just read a book.
You reclaimed a part of yourself.
You made space to tell the truth.
You chose courage over numbness.
You whispered "maybe" where there was once only "never."

And that is everything.

You're no longer waiting to be rescued.
You're no longer silencing your needs to be lovable.

You're no longer hiding the parts of you that are messy, real, growing, radiant.

You are walking forward, head high, heart open, voice clear.

And wherever your story goes from here...
You don't have to do it all alone anymore.

You've found yourself again.
And she is powerful.

Let's keep going.

You're just getting started.

Thank you for reading. If you enjoyed this book, or found it helpful, please take a moment to leave a review with the retailer where the book was published. As a new author, a review means everything!

Chapter 18
Your Empowered Toolkit

T his book was written to speak to your soul, but also to serve your real life.

In these pages, you've faced truths, felt big emotions, and re-imagined what your future could look like. But healing doesn't just happen in the heart, it happens in the hands. That's why every chapter in this book includes an interactive tool, worksheet, or reflection to help you take the next small, meaningful step forward.

This section gathers those tools in one place.

You'll find the printable versions of these worksheets available online at: https://www.novanepublishing.com/sefi-wells#book-resilient

The pages that follow contain the instructions included with each worksheet—offering guidance, clarity, and encouragement.

Use them however and whenever you need:

- Flip to a section after reading a chapter that stirred something.

- Print out pages and post them where they'll keep you grounded.

- Revisit exercises monthly to see how far you've come.

There's no wrong way to use this space, only your way.

Whether it's five quiet minutes with a journal, or a full hour to sit with your thoughts, **this toolkit is here for one purpose**:

To help you put your healing into motion.

You are not just reading a story; you are writing your own.

Let's keep going

Worksheet 1: Where Am I Right Now?

Chapter 1

Take a quiet moment and answer each prompt without editing.
There are no wrong answers.

1. What am I carrying right now that no one else sees?

2. When was the last time I felt supported? What did that look or feel like?

3. What do I wish someone would say to me today?

4. What am I most proud of, even if no one else sees it?

Worksheet 2: The Version of Me I Miss... and the One I Want to Become

Chapter 2

1. What parts of myself have I hidden or forgotten?

2. What did I love about myself before life became about survival?

3. Who do I want to become now, just for me?

4. What's one small thing I can do this week to reconnect with that version of me?

Worksheet 3: My Load Audit

Chapter 3

Draw three columns labeled: **Mental Load | Emotional Load | Physical Tasks**

List everything you carry in each category. Circle the three items that weigh the heaviest on you right now.

Worksheet 4: Permission to Feel

Chapter 4

Write the sentence below, then complete it as many times as you need:

"Today, I give myself permission to feel..."

Examples:

- Today, I give myself permission to feel tired without guilt.

- Today, I give myself permission to feel proud of how far I've come.

Worksheet 5: The Guilt Inventory

Chapter 5

      1. What do I often feel guilty about?

      2. Where did that guilt come from (family, culture, self)?

      3. Is this guilt helping me grow or just hurting me?

      4. What guilt am I ready to release?

Worksheet 6: Rewrite Your Inner Dialogue

Chapter 6

List 3 critical or unkind thoughts you often have:

    1.

    2.

    3.

Now, write a compassionate truth that can replace each one:

    1.

    2.

    3.

Worksheet 7: My Rhythm Map

Chapter 7

Use this space to outline a realistic daily/weekly rhythm that honors your energy, not just your to-do list. Include time blocks for: rest, movement, connection, work, and care.

Worksheet 8: My 'Enough' Budget

Chapter 8

Monthly survival baseline:

- Housing $_____

- Utilities $_____

- Groceries $_____

- Childcare $_____

- Transportation $_____

- Debt minimums $_____

- Other needs $_____

Reflection: What beliefs do I hold about money? Which ones am I ready to rewrite?

Worksheet 9: One Strong Parent Plan

Chapter 9

1. What boundaries do I want to hold with love and consistency?

2. How can I explain rules with both firmness and empathy?

3. What do I want my child to feel when they come to me in struggle?

Worksheet 10: The Things That Light Me Up

Chapter 10

Make a list of things—big or small—that energize or inspire you. Return to this list weekly.

Worksheet 11: What I Want in a Partner Now

Chapter 11

1. What did I learn from my past relationships?

2. What qualities now matter most in a partner?

3. What behaviors, red flags, or dynamics will I never tolerate again?

4. How do I want to feel in love?

Worksheet 12: Micro-Joys & Rest Tracker

Chapter 12

Create a weekly tracker with space for:

- One joyful moment per day

- One act of rest or restoration per day

Example:

Day | Joy | Rest

Mon | Had a chat with a friend | Sat outside for 10 minutes

Worksheet 13: Where to Look for Real Support

Chapter 13

1. Who makes me feel safe, seen, or supported?

2. Where might I find new, healthy connections (online, in-person, local groups)?

3. What small step can I take this week to reach out?

Worksheet 14: Family Resilience Toolkit

Chapter 14

1. What emotional tools do I want to teach my children?

2. What does emotional safety look like in our home?

3. How can we create rituals that build connection and stability?

Worksheet 15: Legacy Letters

Chapter 15

Write a letter to:

Your past self – to honor what she survived.

Your children – to share what you hope they carry forward.

Worksheet 16: Design Your Empowered Life Vision
Chapter 16

What does a peaceful, grounded, joy-filled life look like to me now?

- Emotionally:

- Physically:

- Socially:

- Financially:

- Spiritually:

What small step can I take this week to bring that vision to life?

Worksheet 17: I Am That Woman Manifesto

Chapter 17

Complete or rewrite this bold truth in your own words:

I am a woman who...

I am no longer available for...

I choose...

I release...

I am becoming...

Print. Speak. Return to it every time you forget who you are.

Acknowledgements

Thank you, Jeffrey for providing formatting and artwork, and for designing the amazing cover. Thank you to everyone who made this possible. You know who you are.

About the author

Sefi Wells writes for the woman who carries the world on her shoulders, and still dares to dream of something more.

A mother, creator, and advocate for emotional resilience, Sefi knows firsthand the journey from burnout to hope. Her writing offers a lifeline to single mothers who are ready to heal, to breathe again, and to rebuild a life that feels like their own.

Resilient Heartbeats is her love letter to every woman who has ever doubted herself, reminding them that their strength was never broken, only awaiting rediscovery.

Also by

.

www.ingramcontent.com/pod-product-compliance
Lightning Source LLC
Chambersburg PA
CBHW071403120626
46546CB00002B/796